C000192904

VIz
WIGWATCHING

BOXTREE

FOREWORD
BY TV STAR JEREMY CLARKSON, STAR OF TV'S 'CLARKSON'

I've been lucky enough to visit many strange and beautiful lands whilst filming for the telly, but no tropical sunset can compare to the sight of a man with a badly thatched roof.

One of my favourite sightings happened during a plane flight over Texas, where I was able to spend a good hour marvelling at the head of the man in front. His normal hair was a browny blonde, but that obviously hadn't stopped him going into the shop and saying, "I'll take the bright carrot coloured one please, and make sure it doesn't quite reach down to what's left of my hair." How we laughed and sniggered as the plane bounced in the thermals, but that's the point of a wig really. You can be down, you can have lost your job, your home and your family, but nothing perks a man up quite like the sight of a tip top toupe.

One day boffins will surely crack the problem of the foolproof rug, but until then I hope this innocent pastime continues to give you as much pleasure as it has me.

First published 2002 by Boxtree
an imprint of Pan Macmillan Ltd
Pan Macmillan, 20 New Wharf Road, London N1 9RR
Basingstoke and Oxford
Associated companies throughout the world
www.panmacmillan.com

ISBN 0 7522 1506 X

9 8 7 6 5 4 3 2

A CIP catalogue record for this book is available from
the British Library.

Printed by Proost, Belgium

CONTENTS

If you enjoy laughing at the
nylons in this book, then you'll love
laughing at the musical

WORLD WIDE WIGS

every day... on your PC

Visit the Viz website at

www.viz.co.uk

and download your completely free

WORLD WIDE WIGS
SCREENSAVER

SYRUP SPOTTERS

This book would not have been possible without the tireless efforts of the Viz Syrup Spotters, to whom all of us should be truly grateful. They are, however, too numerous to mention.
So we're not going to bother.

If you have spotted a wig and would like to have it published for others to enjoy without any acknowledgement, send it to

Viz Syrup Spotting
PO Box 1PT
Newcastle upon Tyne
NE99 1PT

or by email to syrups@viz.co.uk

CALCULATING A WIG'S I.Q

Each of the Irish jigs in this book has been awarded an I.Q. (Irish Quotient), an overall score reflecting its risibility. Marks out of 10 are given to a wig in five key categories; these scores are then combined to calculate its I.Q. Thus, the maximum possible I.Q. is one of 50.

As a rule of thumb, a normal comedy wig spotted on a middle-aged uncle at a wedding or on the head of a National Express coach driver will have an I.Q. beween 30 and 40.

The categories are:

Colour mismatch The chromatological disparity between the hairpiece and the wearer's surviving visible hair.

Texture discrepancy The qualitative surface inconsistency between human hair and nylon fibres.

Join noticeability The starkness of the wig/head boundary demarcation.

Shadow castation A visual measure of the amount the wig sits proud of the cranium.

Bleeding obviousness A subjectively sanguine assessment of the manifest conspicuousness of the hairpiece.

OLDEN SYRUPS

the early days
of the Viz Rugs Gallery

Colour mismatch...........4
Texture discrepancy.........6
Join noticeabilty................8
Shadow castation.............3
Bleeding obviousness......7
I.Q....................28

Colour mismatch..............4
Texture discrepancy.........6
Join noticeabilty................9
Shadow castation.............6
Bleeding obviousness......8
I.Q....................32

Colour mismatch.............9
Texture discrepancy.........5
Join noticeabilty..............8
Shadow castation.............7
Bleeding obviousness......8

I.Q.....................37

Colour mismatch.............9
Texture discrepancy.........4
Join noticeabilty..............7
Shadow castation.............6
Bleeding obviousness......8

I.Q.....................34

Colour mismatch.............4
Texture discrepancy.........4
Join noticeabilty.............9
Shadow castation...........9
Bleeding obviousness.......9

I.Q.....................35

Colour mismatch.............9
Texture discrepancy.........9
Join noticeabilty.............9
Shadow castation...........9
Bleeding obviousness......10

I.Q.....................46

Colour mismatch.............6
Texture discrepancy..........5
Join noticeabilty............8
Shadow castation.............9
Bleeding obviousness.........7

I.Q....................35

Colour mismatch.............9
Texture discrepancy..........7
Join noticeabilty...........10
Shadow castation............10
Bleeding obviousness........10

I.Q....................46

Colour mismatch	4
Texture discrepancy	5
Join noticeabilty	9
Shadow castation	9
Bleeding obviousness	9
I.Q.	**36**

Colour mismatch	10
Texture discrepancy	8
Join noticeabilty	10
Shadow castation	9
Bleeding obviousness	10
I.Q.	**47**

Colour mismatch..............10
Texture discrepancy..........9
Join noticeabilty.............10
Shadow castation.............10
Bleeding obviousness......10

I.Q..................49

TOP TOUPS

hairpiece portraits

Wig It has been estimated that over the course of a year, a rug-wearer with plastic soled shoes generates enough static electricity in his toupee to power a town the size of Peterborough for a week. **Factz**

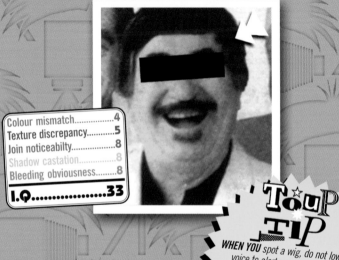

Colour mismatch	4
Texture discrepancy	5
Join noticeabilty	8
Shadow castation	8
Bleeding obviousness	8
I.Q	**33**

TOUP TIP

WHEN YOU spot a wig, do not lower your voice to alert your companions, as rugsters are always alert to whispered conversations and sniggering. Instead, simply nudge your companions in the ribs, widen your eyes and nod in the direction of the wearer.

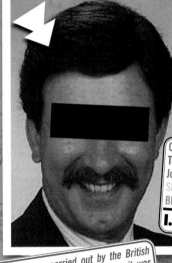

Colour mismatch	3
Texture discrepancy	6
Join noticeabilty	3
Shadow castation	2
Bleeding obviousness	4
I.Q.	**18**

Wig **Factz** In a survey carried out by the British Passenger Transport Executive, it was discovered that almost 78% of train drivers wear some sort of wig, whilst a massive 98% of their coach driving counterparts also sport a hairpiece.

Colour mismatch.............4
Texture discrepancy...........9
Join noticeabilty.............7
Shadow castation.............7
Bleeding obviousness.........8

I.Q..................35

Wig In 1820, the Nantucket whaler Essex was sunk in the Pacific after being struck amidships by an enormous bald sperm whale. It was first thought to be an unprovoked attack, but later accounts by survivors suggested that the beast may have become enraged by the taunts of the sailors who were pointing and sniggering at its bright orange seaweed toupee.

Factz

Colour mismatch.............6
Texture discrepancy..........4
Join noticeabilty..................9
Shadow castation.............6
Bleeding obviousness.........9

I.Q...................34

21

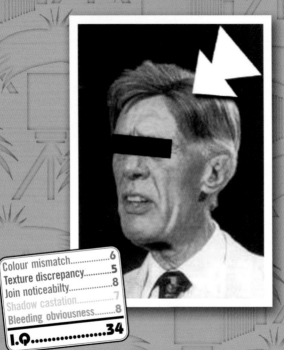

Colour mismatch................6
Texture discrepancy...........5
Join noticeabilty.............8
Shadow castation..............7
Bleeding obviousness..........8

I.Q....................34

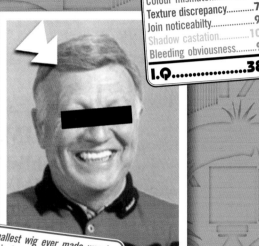

Wig The smallest wig ever made was just half an inch across and fashioned from the bright orange abdomen of a bumble bee. It was worn by the world's smallest man, Calvin Phillips, for his sister's wedding in 1973. Sadly, on the morning of the marriage, Phillips, hung over from quaffing fifteen thimbles-full of beer, put the wig on upside down and stang himself to death. **Factz**

Wig During the war, baldies found it impossible to get wigs on the home front, as all available toupees were sent to slapheaded soldiers on the front. But refusing to let Hitler have the last laugh, bald Britons made do and mended, gluing everything from dead squirrels to mop-heads onto their plucky pates.

Factz

Colour mismatch	7
Texture discrepancy	8
Join noticeabilty	10
Shadow castation	8
Bleeding obviousness	10
I.Q.	**43**

TOUP TIP

A RAILWAY station is a good place to spot wigs, as many people will be coming and going, and train drivers will almost certainly be wearing rugs. The harsh lighting is also good for casting a shadow where the wig stands proud of the scalp. Rug photographers will be mistaken for innocent trainspotters, and will be able to snap away without alarming their quarry.

Colour mismatch	7
Texture discrepancy	8
Join noticeabilty	6
Shadow castation	4
Bleeding obviousness	7
I.Q.	**32**

Wig In Greek mythology, the fabled Golden Fleece which was sought by Jason and the Argonauts was in fact an enormous ginger wig. It was stolen from the pate of the God Titan by Perseus who snatched it after turning himself into a giant eagle. It was said that whoever wore the wig would be granted the illusion of eternal youth, but at a cost. Wherever he went he would be sniggered and pointed at behind his back. **Factz**

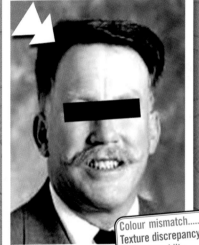

Colour mismatch.............10
Texture discrepancy...........9
Join noticeabilty................9
Shadow castation.............9
Bleeding obviousness.......10

I.Q....................47

27

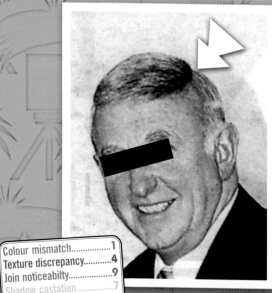

Colour mismatch..............1
Texture discrepancy..........4
Join noticeabilty.............9
Shadow castation.............7
Bleeding obviousness.........7

I.Q...................28

28

Colour mismatch	6
Texture discrepancy	10
Join noticeabilty	8
Shadow castation	9
Bleeding obviousness	9
I.Q.	**44**

Wig Scientists in Japan are developing robotic headlice. These tiny electronic insects, looking exactly like ordinary nits, will be able to survive the harsh conditions found within a toupee, fuelling themselves with small flakes of nylon. They will itch and will be squashable on the side of the sink just like their real-life counterparts. There is only drawback - they will cost $300,000 each, that's over $10 million for an average head infestation. **Factz**

Colour mismatch	10
Texture discrepancy	9
Join noticeabilty	9
Shadow castation	9
Bleeding obviousness	10
I.Q.	**47**

TOUP TIP

IN THE same way that birdwatchers construct reed hides from which to observe waterfowl, rug watchers can construct a hideout of oak panelling and situate it in the assembly rooms of their local town council, a common haven for wig-wearers.

BIG WIGS

ceremonial headwear for
public appearances

Colour mismatch.................3
Texture discrepancy............8
Join noticeabilty.................8
Shadow castation................9
Bleeding obviousness..........8

I.Q.....................36

32

Colour mismatch	5
Texture discrepancy	8
Join noticeabilty	8
Shadow castation	9
Bleeding obviousness	9
I.Q.	**39**

Wig The earliest reference to a wig is found in the Bible: 'And lo, they brought unto Jesus Pethuel of Aramathea, who was afflicted with baldness. And Jesus bent down and did take up a handful of crinkly orange straw and place it on the head of Pethuel of Aramathea, saying, Take this straw, for it will be your hair. And the disciples looked on, and did nudge each other and great was their sniggering. And Pethuel cared not, for he knew not that they knew it was not real.' **Factz** - Geronimo Chapter 6.

Colour mismatch	7
Texture discrepancy	10
Join noticeabilty	8
Shadow castation	9
Bleeding obviousness	9

I.Q 43

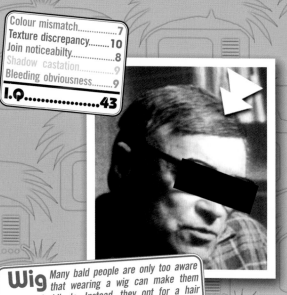

Wig Many bald people are only too aware that wearing a wig can make them objects of ridicule. Instead, they opt for a hair transplant, an incredibly painful process whereby small tufts of hair are removed from between their buttocks and planted in a geometrical grid formation on their foreheads. The overall effect is that of a large winnity toothbrush, and the transplantee is often to be seen wearing a hat. **Factz**

Colour mismatch	10
Texture discrepancy	9
Join noticeabilty	10
Shadow castation	9
Bleeding obviousness	10
I.Q.	**48**

35

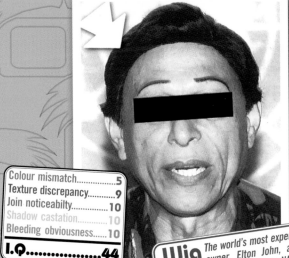

Colour mismatch	5
Texture discrepancy	9
Join noticeabilty	10
Shadow castation	10
Bleeding obviousness	10
I.Q.	**44**

Wig The world's most expensive wig cost its owner, Elton John, a mammoth £30 million. The rug was woven from NASA grade teflon by a team of 700 trichologists and hair stylists, and took three years to make. When in place, the resultant hairpiece is absolutely undetectable, **Factz** unless you look at the top of his head.

Colour mismatch	6
Texture discrepancy	8
Join noticeabilty	7
Shadow castation	4
Bleeding obviousness	6
I.Q.	**31**

TOUP TIP

ALERT friends to the presence of a wig using a simple pre-arranged code phrase, such as 'there's a stone in my shoe.' For greater accuracy, a simple clock-face reference will indicate the direction, eg. 'there's a stone in my shoe at three o'clock'.

Colour mismatch	3
Texture discrepancy	7
Join noticeabilty	10
Shadow castation	9
Bleeding obviousness	10
I.Q.	**39**

Wig

Ironically, speed ace Donald Campbell's 'lucky' wig cost him his life. Whilst making an attempt on the world water speed record in 1967, Campbell's toupee was sucked from his head and into Bluebird's turbojet intake, causing his fatal crash. His last words, "She's going!" are not, as many people think, a reference to his hydroplane lifting from the water surface due to it hitting its own bow-wave, but in fact refer to his wig coming adrift from his pate.

Factz

Colour mismatch.............4
Texture discrepancy...........5
Join noticeabilty.............10
Shadow castation............10
Bleeding obviousness.........8
I.Q...................37

39

I.Q.....................47

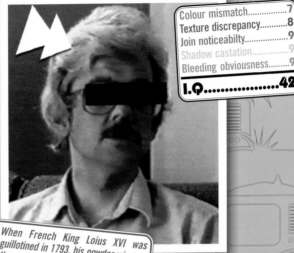

Wig When French King Loius XVI was guillotined in 1793, his powder wig was so large that the executioner feared that his severed head would not fit in the basket. The beheading was delayed and it was feared a suitable basket was not to be found in all of France. The day was saved by pioneer aviators the Montgolfier brothers, Etienne and Joseph, who arrived with the king-sized wicker gondola off their balloon. **Factz**

Colour mismatch..................8
Texture discrepancy..........10
Join noticeabilty................10
Shadow castation................10
Bleeding obviousness......10

I.Q....................48

Wig

Retired US businessman Hank Oyster-burger had reason to thank his lucky wig when he fell off his yacht whilst fishing for blue marlin 20 miles off Florida's Cocoa Beach. As night fell, rescuers had all but given up hope of finding him alive when his fluorescent ginger toupee showed up on satellite photographs, enabling them to pinpoint his position. Coastguards found the 82-year-old still clinging to his toupee, the bouyancy of which had kept him afloat for almost 18 hours. **Factz**

Colour mismatch.............8
Texture discrepancy...........9
Join noticeabilty...............10
Shadow castation.............10
Bleeding obviousness......10

I.Q....................47

43

TOUP TIP

IN THE same way that hairdressing and air stewarding attract a high proportion of gay men, wig wearers are irresistably drawn to certain lines of work. Look out for them in local government, broadcast media and the Salvation Army. Don't bother looking for them at Van der Graaff generator factories or wind tunnel testing plants.

Colour mismatch	9
Texture discrepancy	8
Join noticeabilty	10
Shadow castation	7
Bleeding obviousness	9
I.Q.	**43**

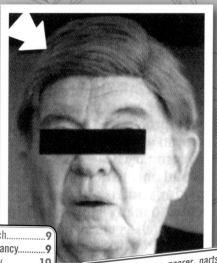

Colour mismatch	9
Texture discrepancy	9
Join noticeabilty	10
Shadow castation	10
Bleeding obviousness	10
I.Q	**48**

Wig *In many poorer parts of the world, people sell their hair for export to the west to be turned into exclusive 'natural' wigs. However, before they are sold, these human hairpieces are treated with a special mixture of chemicals that gives every strand of hair the texture and appearance of Bri-nylon.* **Factz**

Colour mismatch	9
Texture discrepancy	8
Join noticeabilty	9
Shadow castation	10
Bleeding obviousness	10
I.Q.	**46**

Wig In Georgian London, the fashion amongst gentlemen was for large and elaborate wigs, the larger and more elaborate the better. So much so, that it was quite common for families of fleas or even mice to be living in them without the owner knowing. When society dandy Beau Brummell died in 1840, his huge wig was discovered to be home to 100 sparrows, 35 rats, 10 rabbits, 250 assorted bats, 6 foxes, a pair of badgers and a half ton polar bear. **Factz**

47

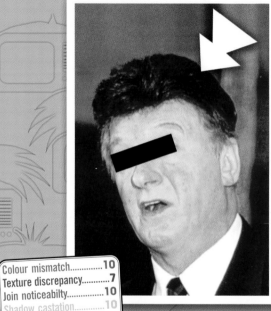

Colour mismatch............... 10
Texture discrepancy............ 7
Join noticeabilty................ 10
Shadow castation............. 10
Bleeding obviousness........ 9

I.Q....................46

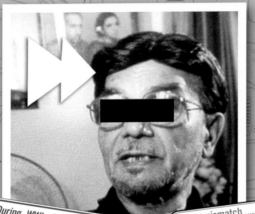

Wig

During WWI, German ace Baron von Richthofen struck fear into the hearts of British pilots. But his nickname of The Red Baron had nothing to do with the colour of his Fokker triplane - it was because the vain flier sported a bright ginger wig. His British WWII counterpart Sir Douglas Bader was also a rugster. He was famous for his distinctive rusty tin wig which he wore after being scalped when he was catapulted through the propellor of his Spitfire.

Factz

Colour mismatch	6
Texture discrepancy	9
Join noticeabilty	9
Shadow castation	9
Bleeding obviousness	9
I.Q.	**42**

Wig For the filming of the 1974 Hollywood blockbuster Earthquake, Universal Studios technicians developed an extra-strong wig glue that secured star Charlton Heston's toupee to his scalp during the action scenes. The glue proved so good that 27 years later, Heston's wig is still stuck firmly to his head. **Factz**

Colour mismatch	4
Texture discrepancy	6
Join noticeabilty	9
Shadow castation	8
Bleeding obviousness	9
I.Q.	**36**

TÒUP TIP

EVEN the housebound can still enjoy the pleasures of wigwatching. Local newspapers are a fruitful hunting ground, as any picture of a group of people handing over a large cheque will invariably contain at least 2 rugheads. In addition, Crimewatch UK generally features 3 or 4 Detective Inspectors sporting their best Irish jigs for their 15 minutes of fame.

Colour mismatch	8
Texture discrepancy	8
Join noticeabilty	10
Shadow castation	9
Bleeding obviousness	9
I.Q.	**44**

51

Colour mismatch..............8
Texture discrepancy..........10
Join noticeabilty.............7
Shadow castation.............8
Bleeding obviousness.........9

I.Q......................42

52

Colour mismatch.............10
Texture discrepancy.........8
Join noticeabilty.............9
Shadow castation............9
Bleeding obviousness.......10

I.Q...................46

Wig After the Battle of the Little Big Horn, General George W. Custard had reason to thank his wig for saving his life. As Custard fell wounded to the ground, Chief Sitting Bull stepped forward and grabbed his hair. With a single swipe of his tomahawk , the short-sighted Apachee removed the general's wig, and thinking it was his scalp, ran off to perform a victory dance. Custard escaped unhurt, but wigless. **Factz**

53

Wig We often tell someone to 'keep their hair on' when they are about to punch or glass us in a pub. The phrase originally arose from duelling ettiquette, where the duellists would customarily hand their coats and wigs to their seconds to hold. Before the fight commenced, the referee would give the two protagonists a final chance to avert bloodshed with the phrase: 'Sirs, will you fight to the death, or will you keep your hair on?' **factz**

Colour mismatch	6
Texture discrepancy	10
Join noticeabilty	10
Shadow castation	6
Bleeding obviousness	10

I.Q. 42

SYRUPTICIOUS SNAPS

candid photos of wigs
about their daily business

TOUP TIP

IF YOU suspect a neighbour of being a rug top, try and catch him unawares. Kick a football into his garden at 6 o'clock in the morning, then knock on his door to ask for it back. He would never appear at the door without his wig, but in his bleary-eyed daze he may well have put it on badly, perhaps even back to front.

Colour mismatch	9
Texture discrepancy	9
Join noticeabilty	10
Shadow castation	7
Bleeding obviousness	9
I.Q.	**44**

Colour mismatch	10
Texture discrepancy	8
Join noticeabilty	9
Shadow castation	9
Bleeding obviousness	10
I.Q.	**46**

Wig It isn't just silly middle-aged men and TV chat show hosts who wear wigs. Rug-tops are common through all walks of life, including the world of sport. In the 2001-2002 season there were no less than 14 players in the Barclaycard Premiership league who wore some form of hairpiece, including 2 who turned out for England. Needless to say, none of them ever headed the ball.

Factz

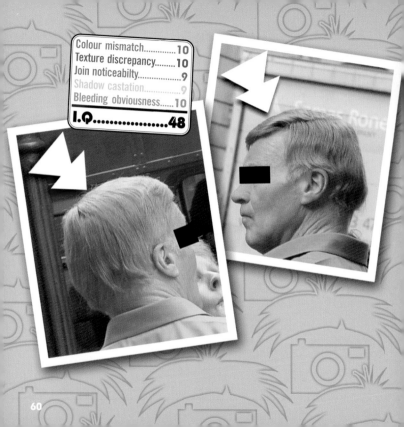

Colour mismatch..............10
Texture discrepancy.........10
Join noticeabilty..............9
Shadow castation..............9
Bleeding obviousness......10

I.Q.................48

TOUP TIP

AT SOCIAL functions, toups may be snapped using the decoy method. The photographer uses an accomplice who poses 'innocently' next to his quarry. The decoy is then cropped out of the resultant prints.

Colour mismatch	7
Texture discrepancy	7
Join noticeabilty	8
Shadow castation	8
Bleeding obviousness	9
I.Q.	**41**

Wig In 1951, Howard Pratt took his wife Dolly on a day trip to Blackpool. While they were standing on the end of the pier, a sudden gust of wind got under his toupee and blew it out to sea. In 1976, and now living in Australia, the couple went to a seafood restaurant in Melbourne. Upon cutting into his fried sea bass, Howard saw a flash of ginger, and was amazed to discover his lost toupee, none the worse for its 25 year, 12,000 mile oddysey! **Factz**

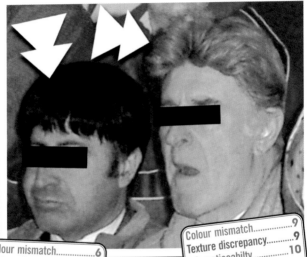

Colour mismatch.............6
Texture discrepancy.............7
Join noticeabilty.............8
Shadow castation.............7
Bleeding obviousness.............9
I.Q.....................37

Colour mismatch.............9
Texture discrepancy.............9
Join noticeabilty.............10
Shadow castation.............9
Bleeding obviousness.......10
I.Q.....................47

Colour mismatch..................8
Texture discrepancy.........10
Join noticeabilty................10
Shadow castation.............10
Bleeding obviousness.......10

I.Q...................48

64

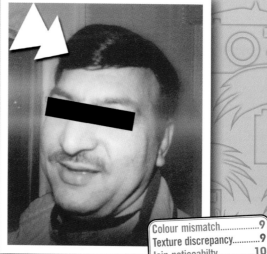

Colour mismatch.............9
Texture discrepancy..........9
Join noticeabilty............10
Shadow castation............4
Bleeding obviousness........8

I.Q.................42

66

Colour mismatch	9
Texture discrepancy	10
Join noticeabilty	10
Shadow castation	8
Bleeding obviousness	10

I.Q. 47

Wig Like normal people, religious individuals can go prematurely bald. Ecclesiastical wig shops offer 'Tonsure Toupees' - special doughnut-shaped wigs for monks, as well as 'Vicar's Strips' - thin bands of fake white hair that attach above curate's ears and around the backs of their heads. **Factz**

Colour mismatch	7
Texture discrepancy	9
Join noticeabilty	8
Shadow castation	9
Bleeding obviousness	9
I.Q.	**42**

WIGS YOU WERE HERE

sunny syrups
around the world

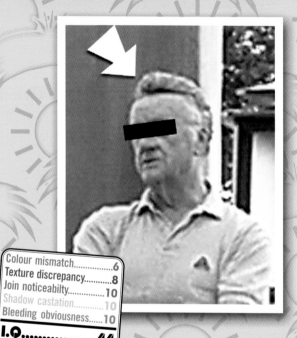

Colour mismatch.................6
Texture discrepancy..........8
Join noticeabilty..............10
Shadow castation.............10
Bleeding obviousness.......10

I.Q....................44

70

Colour mismatch.............3
Texture discrepancy.............8
Join noticeabilty.............10
Shadow castation.............10
Bleeding obviousness.......10

I.Q.................41

73

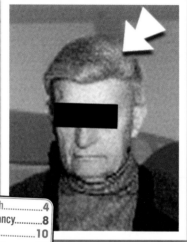

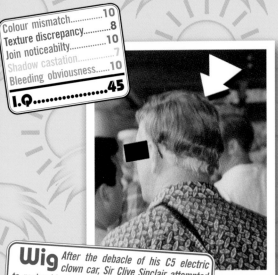

Colour mismatch	10
Texture discrepancy	8
Join noticeabilty	10
Shadow castation	7
Bleeding obviousness	10
I.Q.	**45**

Wig After the debacle of his C5 electric clown car, Sir Clive Sinclair attempted to revive his fortunes by inventing a revolutionary wig. The Sinclair Toupex 2000, the world's first self-balding wig was launched in February 1985. Mimicking a real scalp, the hairline on the Toupex 2000 gradually receded until, after about 20 years, all that remained was the backing canvas 'pate'. The idea never caught on, and only one **Factz** was ever sold.

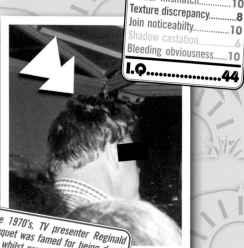

Colour mismatch	**10**
Texture discrepancy	**8**
Join noticeabilty	**10**
Shadow castation	6
Bleeding obviousness	**10**
I.Q.	**44**

Wig

Factz

In the 1970's, TV presenter Reginald Bosanquet was famed for being drunk and wearing a wig whilst presenting 'News at Ten'. Whilst announcing an earthquake in Mexico, he hiccoughed and his toupee slipped over his eyes. Unable to see the autocue, he decided to fill in by singing 'Danny Boy' at the top of his voice. Farcical scenes ensued for several minutes as a team of make-up ladies battled to re-align the offending hairpiece.

Colour mismatch..............10
Texture discrepancy..........10
Join noticeabilty.............10
Shadow castation...........10
Bleeding obviousness.......10

I.Q....................50

"The King of Wigs"

TOUP TIP

MANY rug-heads keep a wig for best, so a big social occasion provides happy hunting for the keen wigspotter. Keep your eyes peeled at weddings, Christenings, funerals, family get-togethers and at recordings of TV's 'The Price is Right'.

Colour mismatch.................2
Texture discrepancy...........8
Join noticeabilty...............6
Shadow castation..............3
Bleeding obviousness.........8

I.Q.....................27

I.Q................41

Wig

Everyone knows that Van Gogh cut his ear off. What fewer people know is that he did it because he wore a wig! Whilst painting a self-portrait in his room at Arles in 1888, Vincent noticed the label from his ginger wig was sticking out. Trying to remove the offending item with his pallette knife, he slipped, completely severing his earlobe. The following year he went out into a nearby field and attempted to shoot the label off, with fatal consequences.

Factz

Colour mismatch	10
Texture discrepancy	10
Join noticeabilty	10
Shadow castation	9
Bleeding obviousness	10
I.Q.	**49**

Toup Tip

A SMALL camera, mounted sideways on top of an old 35mm camera makes an ideal rugsnapping device. The photograher can stand alongside his subject, face foward and click away, taking close-up shots without arousing any suspicion.

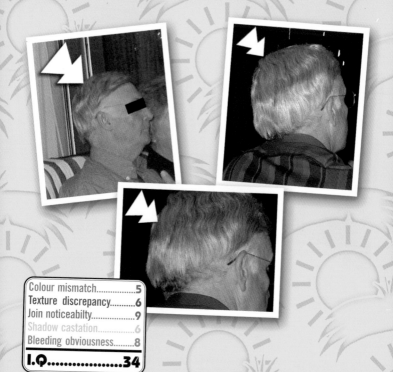

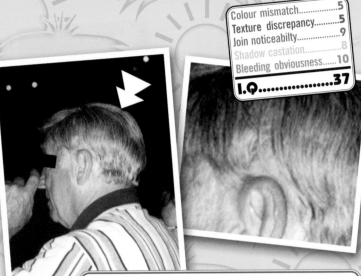

Wig Wigs have often been pivotal in the course of history. At the battle of Hastings in 1066, King Harold's toupee slid forward when his horse slipped on a cowpat. Tilting his head back to adjust it, he was struck square in the eye by William the Conqueror's arrow, changing the course of British history. In the Bayeux tapestry, Harold's wig can still clearly be seen, though over the past 900 years the original bright ginger threads have faded to a dull brown. **Factz**

82

Colour mismatch...........7
Texture discrepancy..........9
Join noticeabilty............9
Shadow castation............10
Bleeding obviousness..........9

I.Q.....................44

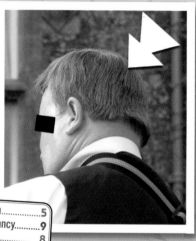

Colour mismatch....................5
Texture discrepancy............9
Join noticeabilty....................8
Shadow castation....................7
Bleeding obviousness.............8

I.Q.....................37

Colour mismatch	9
Texture discrepancy	9
Join noticeabilty	9
Shadow castation	9
Bleeding obviousness	9
I.Q	**45**

Wig Chimpanzees (Pan troglodytes) share 95% of their genes with human beings, and one of those genes codes for male patterned baldness. When a male chimpanzee begins to recede, he often disguises the fact by wearing a crude wig, made from the orange head feathers of the Sulphur crested cockatoo (Cacatua galerita). Ironically the only ginger primate, the orang-utan (Simia satyrus) makes his wig from the jet black feathers of the Great Black palm Cockatoo (Probosciger aterrimus). **Factz**

Wig William Shakespeare is famed throughout the world for his historical plays, tragedies and sonnets. But earlier in his career, he wrote a series of low farces, one of which is about a man who gets his wig caught in his sister-in-law's chastity belt just as the bishop turns up unexpectedly for tea. The play, entitled 'Mind my Rug, Madam!' was performed only once, in 1584, and no record of it survives. **Factz**

Colour mismatch	9
Texture discrepancy	10
Join noticeabilty	10
Shadow castation	10
Bleeding obviousness	10
I.Q	**49**

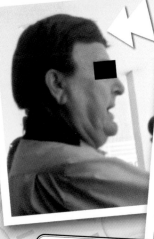

Colour mismatch	6
Texture discrepancy	7
Join noticeabilty	7
Shadow castation	7
Bleeding obviousness	7
I.Q	**34**

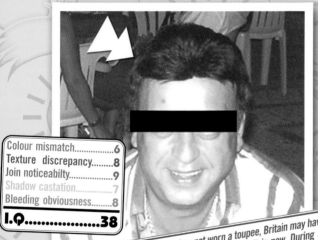

Colour mismatch	6
Texture discrepancy	8
Join noticeabilty	9
Shadow castation	7
Bleeding obviousness	8
I.Q.	**38**

Wig Had Guy Fawkes not worn a toupee, Britain may have been a very different place today than it is now. During a random inspection of the House of Commons cellars in 1642, a sharp-eyed guard spotted what he thought was a fairground gonk behind a barrel, and decided to take it home for his daughter. It turned out to be the gunpowder plotter - complete with garishly coloured wig. The bright orange fireworks which we explode every year on November 5th commemorate Fawkes's hairpiece faux pas, and celebrate his plot to blow up **Factz** parliament and the royal family.

THE HAIR-MARE BUNCH

combovers, brillo swopes
& general disasters

Wig In medieval England, wealth was denoted by the fanciness of a person's wig, hence the term 'Bigwig'. Except in Nottingham where, thanks to Robin Hood and his band of merry outlaws, large wigs were stolen from the rich and given to the local poor people. **Factz**

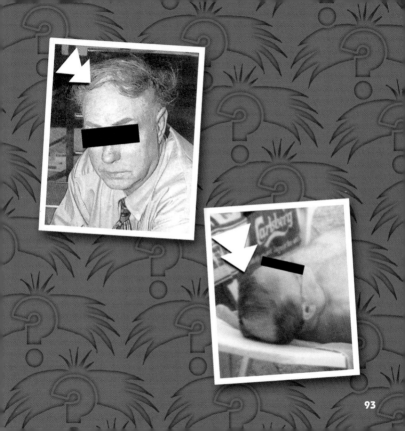